Spotter's Guide to
AIRLINERS
AND AIRLINES

Civil aircraft of the world

Alan Wright

Contents

Illustrations by Tony Gibbons
Additional artwork by Joseph McEwan
Designed by Kim Blundell
Edited by Lisa Watts

Photographs provided by airlines and
aircraft manufacturers and by
Alan Wright, G. L. Lawrence and
C. P. Wright

First published in 1980 by Usborne
Publishing Ltd, 20 Garrick Street,
London WC2 9BJ, England.

Copyright © 1980 Usborne
Publishing Ltd
Published in Australia by Rigby
Publishing Ltd, Adelaide, Sydney,
Melbourne, Brisbane.

GRAFICAS REUNIDAS, S A.
Av de Aragón, 56   Madrid 27

How to use this book

This book is a simple guide to help you identify airliners and the airlines they fly with. An airliner is a plane which flies on a regular route, carrying passengers or cargo.

The aircraft are arranged in five groups, according to the number and type of engines they have. These different groups are explained on page 4.

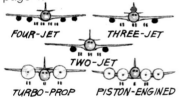

FOUR-JET   THREE-JET   TWO-JET   TURBO-PROP   PISTON-ENGINED

When you see a plane, first decide which group it belongs to. Then look in the contents list and turn to the right pages for that group of planes.

For each plane there is a coloured photograph and two black silhouette pictures showing the shape from the side and below. The pictures are not to scale.

REGISTRATION NUMBER

If you are quite close, or have binoculars, you may be able to read the registration number of the plane. Then you can look the number up on pages 56–57 and find out where the plane is registered.

AIR CANADA

To find out which airline a plane is flying with, turn to the second part of the book. There are pictures of planes in the colours of 65 airlines, with hints for airline spotting on page 35.

Beside each picture of a plane there is a circle to tick when you spot it. After a day out spotting you can add up your score on the scorecards at the back of the book.

Going plane spotting

Most large airports have special viewing balconies where you can go to watch the planes taking-off and landing. At small airports and airstrips you can often get a good view from outside the boundary fences. Make sure you do not trespass on airport property. You may not have to go to an airport to spot planes though. If you live nearby you can probably identify some of the aircraft as they fly overhead.

What to take

As well as this book it is a good idea to take a notebook, pencil and a pair of binoculars if you have some. You can take a camera but the planes will come out very small unless you are very near them.

Write down the names, airlines and, if possible, registration numbers of planes you spot. Look out for planes with special names, such as the British Airways 747 called "Sir Francis Drake".

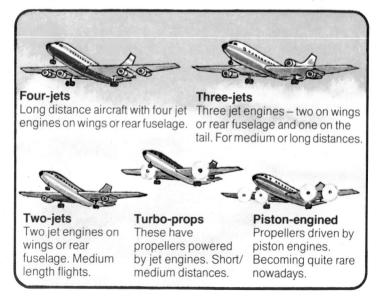

Four-jets
Long distance aircraft with four jet engines on wings or rear fuselage.

Three-jets
Three jet engines – two on wings or rear fuselage and one on the tail. For medium or long distances.

Two-jets
Two jet engines on wings or rear fuselage. Medium length flights.

Turbo-props
These have propellers powered by jet engines. Short/medium distances.

Piston-engined
Propellers driven by piston engines. Becoming quite rare nowadays.

Parts of a plane

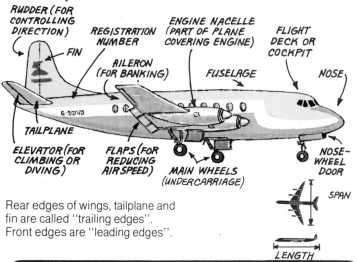

RUDDER (FOR CONTROLLING DIRECTION)

FIN

REGISTRATION NUMBER

AILERON (FOR BANKING)

ENGINE NACELLE (PART OF PLANE COVERING ENGINE)

FUSELAGE

FLIGHT DECK OR COCKPIT

NOSE

TAILPLANE

ELEVATOR (FOR CLIMBING OR DIVING)

FLAPS (FOR REDUCING AIR SPEED)

MAIN WHEELS (UNDERCARRIAGE)

NOSE-WHEEL DOOR

G-AOWD

SPAN

LENGTH

Rear edges of wings, tailplane and fin are called "trailing edges". Front edges are "leading edges".

Points to look out for

To identify an aircraft, first note where the engines are positioned, then look at the shape and position of the wings, tailplane and fin.

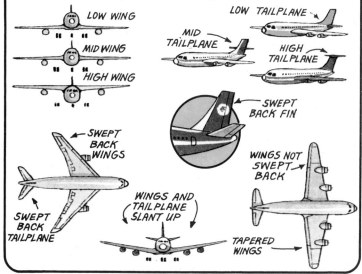

LOW WING

MID WING

HIGH WING

LOW TAILPLANE

MID TAILPLANE

HIGH TAILPLANE

SWEPT BACK FIN

SWEPT BACK WINGS

WINGS NOT SWEPT BACK

SWEPT BACK TAILPLANE

WINGS AND TAILPLANE SLANT UP

TAPERED WINGS

Four-jets

THE 707 AND 720 ARE VERY ALIKE. THEY ALSO LOOK LIKE THE DC-8 BUT HAVE A MORE STREAMLINED NOSE (p.10)

▲ 707 (Boeing, U.S.A.) *
First flew in 1957, with first Atlantic service in 1958. Now no longer produced, but over 750 were built and hundreds are still in service. Largest model carries up to 200 passengers.

Span 44.4m, length 46.6m (Model 320C)
Maximum cruising speed 965kph

Span 40.1m, length 41.6m
Maximum cruising speed 983kph

▲ 720 (Boeing, U.S.A.)
Medium-range jet for 170 people. Looks very like short version of 707, but can often be identified by name near passenger door. First flight 1959. No longer produced, but 154 were built and many are still in service.

* The name of the plane is first, then the manufacturer and the country where it is made.

Four-jets

BULGING ROOF OF FORWARD FUSELAGE

THESE TWO PLANES ARE IN THE MANUFACTURER'S OWN LIVERY

▲ 747 (Boeing, U.S.A.)
Often called "Jumbo-jet", this was the first wide-bodied jet. It went into service 22 January 1970 and over 500 have been sold. Usually equipped for 350 passengers, but can carry up to 500. Look out for cargo version – its nose opens upwards for loading.

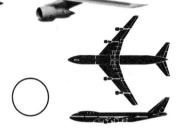

Span 59.6m, length 70.5m
Maximum cruising speed 939kph

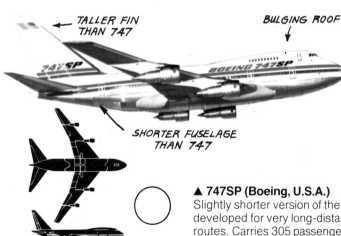

TALLER FIN THAN 747

BULGING ROOF

SHORTER FUSELAGE THAN 747

Span 59.6m, length 56.3m
Maximum cruising speed 935kph

▲ 747SP (Boeing, U.S.A.)
Slightly shorter version of the 747 developed for very long-distance routes. Carries 305 passengers for distances over 10,000km. First operated in 1976, there are now 35 in service with nine airlines.

Four-jets

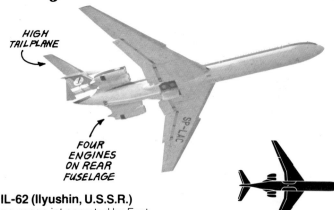

HIGH TAILPLANE

FOUR ENGINES ON REAR FUSELAGE

▲ **IL-62 (Ilyushin, U.S.S.R.)**
Long-range jet operated by East European airlines. Engine and tail position similar to VC-10 (below), but slimmer fuselage. First flown 1963, entered service 1967 and 130 have now been built. Later versions carry 195 passengers.

Span 43.2m, length 53.1m
Maximum cruising speed 920kph

HIGH TAILPLANE

ROUNDED SHAPE

FOUR ENGINES ON REAR FUSELAGE

Span 44.5, length 52.3m (Super)
Maximum cruising speed 914kph

▲ **Super VC-10 (Vickers, BAC, U.K.)**
Only airliner other than IL-62 (above) with four rear-mounted engines. Designed for medium-to-long distance routes, it entered service in 1964. Standard VC-10, of which few remain, is 4m shorter than Super which can carry 174 passengers.

8

Four-jets

BULGES
STICK OUT
BEHIND
WINGS

▲ **Cv 990 Coronado (Convair, U.S.A.)**
Fastest jet airliner other than
Concorde. In Europe, can be seen
in colours of Spantax airline,
operating on holiday charters.
Entered service in 1962. Only 37
built. Carries 106 to 149
passengers. Looks like DC-8
(page 10), but identified by two
bulges on top of each wing.

Span 36.5m, length 42.3m
Maximum cruising speed 990kph

UPRIGHT FIN

TAILPLANE
SLOPES UP

ENGINES ENCLOSED
IN WINGS

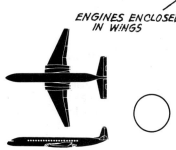

▲ **DH 106 Comet 4 (Hawker
Siddeley, U.K.)**
Developed from early Comets
which were world's first jet
airliners. Comet 4 made the first
transatlantic passenger service on
4 October 1958. Unusual design
with engines enclosed in wings.
Carries about 100 passengers.
Last remaining Comets are
operated by Dan-Air.

Span 32.9m, length 36m
Maximum cruising speed 846kph

Four-jets

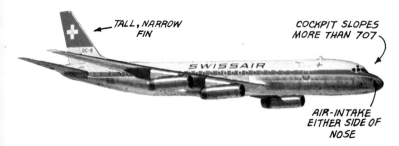

TALL, NARROW FIN

COCKPIT SLOPES MORE THAN 707

SWISSAIR

AIR-INTAKE EITHER SIDE OF NOSE

▲ DC8 (McDonnell Douglas, U.S.A.) Series 10 to 50
Similar shape and size to Boeing 707, but can be recognized by shape of cockpit. Seats 116 to 179. First flew in 1958 and still used on world-wide schedule and charter flights. Freighter version has large cargo door in front fuselage.

Span 43.3m, length 45.7m
Maximum cruising speed 933kph

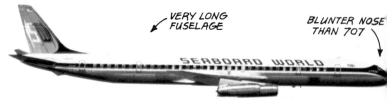

VERY LONG FUSELAGE

BLUNTER NOSE THAN 707

SEABOARD WORLD

Span 45.2m, length 48m (Series 62), 57.1m (Series 61 and 63) Maximum cruising speed 965kph

▲ DC8 (McDonnell Douglas, U.S.A.) Series 60
Easy to recognize by long, thin fuselage. Series 61 is 11.8m longer than earlier DC-8s and can carry 259 passengers. The 62 is only 2m longer, with other modifications to improve performance. The 63 has long fuselage and other improvements. Total of 262 built.

Four-jets

POINTED NOSE (DROOPS DOWN WHEN LANDING AND TAXIING)

SQUARE-SHAPED ENGINE NACELLES

WIDE WINGS CALLED "DELTA-WINGS" (GREEK LETTER DELTA = Δ)

▲ Concorde (BAC/Aerospatiale, U.K./France)

Medium-to-long range supersonic airliner. First flew 2 March 1969. First passenger services from both London and Paris, 21 January 1976. Carries about 120 passengers in slim fuselage. Ten aircraft in service with Air France and British Airways. Production ended with four built but unsold.

Span 25.6m, length 62.1m
Maximum cruising speed 2,179kph

HIGH TAILPLANE

PICTURE SHOWS ARTIST'S IMPRESSION

WINGS SLOPE DOWN

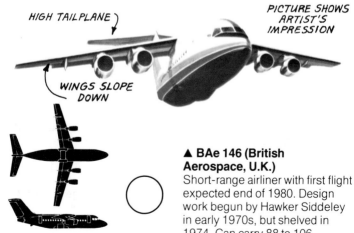

▲ BAe 146 (British Aerospace, U.K.)

Short-range airliner with first flight expected end of 1980. Design work begun by Hawker Siddeley in early 1970s, but shelved in 1974. Can carry 88 to 106 passengers depending on version. No orders yet.

Span 26.3m, length 26.16m
Estimated cruising speed 790kph

Three-jets

BULLET SHAPE ON TOP OF FIN

TYPE NAME ON CENTRE ENGINE

TWO EXHAUST NOZZLES

▲ HS121 Trident 3 (Hawker Siddeley, U.K.)

Carries up to 179 passengers on medium-range flights. In service only with Britain and China. Look out too, for Trident 1 which has a slightly shorter fuselage, and Trident 2 which is very similar. All three have a high tailplane and their type names on the centre engine.

Span 29.9m, length 40m
Maximum cruising speed 967kph

HIGH TAILPLANE

FIN SLOPES BACK MORE THAN TRIDENT'S

EXHAUST NOZZLE

Span 32.9m, length 46.7m
Maximum cruising speed 964kph

▲ 727 (Boeing, U.S.A.)

World's best selling jet airliner for short/medium distances. First flight 1963. Later versions take up to 189 passengers and over 1,700 have been sold. Can be spotted at most airports. Larger than the Tridents and fin slopes back more sharply.

Three-jets

HIGH TAILPLANE

SHARP POINT

▲ Tu-154 (Tupolev, U.S.S.R.)
Medium-range airliner of similar design to Trident and Boeing 727, but longer and slimmer. Carries up to 169 passengers and used mainly by East European airlines. First flight 1968, entered full passenger service in 1972.

POINTS STICKING OUT BEHIND WINGS

Span 37.5m, length 47.9m
Maximum cruising speed 972kph

ENGINE MOULDED INTO FIN

EXHAUST NOZZLE IN REAR FUSELAGE

Span 47.3m, length 54.9m
Maximum cruising speed 990kph

▲ TriStar (Lockheed, U.S.A.)
Wide-bodied airliner able to carry 400 passengers on medium-length flights. Entered service in 1972. Two engines under the wings and third in the rear fuselage with air-intake moulded into fin. Compare with rear engine on DC-10 (page 14).

Three-jets

EXHAUST NOZZLE IN FIN

▲ DC-10 (McDonnell Douglas, U.S.A.)

Similar in size and layout to TriStar (page 13), but note rear engine position in fin. Series 10 entered service in 1971 on U.S. domestic flights. Series 30 designed for intercontinental services. Both types carry 350 passengers.

Span 47.3m (Series 10), 50.4m (Series 30), length 55.3m
Maximum cruising speed 956kph

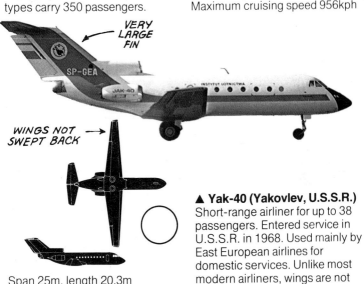

VERY LARGE FIN

WINGS NOT SWEPT BACK →

Span 25m, length 20.3m
Maximum cruising speed 560kph

▲ Yak-40 (Yakovlev, U.S.S.R.)

Short-range airliner for up to 38 passengers. Entered service in U.S.S.R. in 1968. Used mainly by East European airlines for domestic services. Unlike most modern airliners, wings are not swept back.

Two-jets

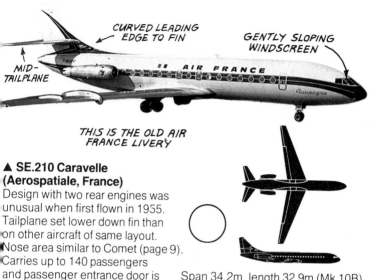

CURVED LEADING EDGE TO FIN

GENTLY SLOPING WINDSCREEN

MID-TAILPLANE

II AIR FRANCE

THIS IS THE OLD AIR FRANCE LIVERY

▲ SE.210 Caravelle (Aerospatiale, France)
Design with two rear engines was unusual when first flown in 1955. Tailplane set lower down fin than on other aircraft of same layout. Nose area similar to Comet (page 9). Carries up to 140 passengers and passenger entrance door is under rear fuselage.

Span 34.2m, length 32.9m (Mk 10B)
Maximum cruising speed 845kph

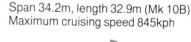

Span 28.5m, length 36.4m (Series 30), 45m (Series 80)
Maximum cruising speed (Srs 30) 909kph

▲ DC-9 (McDonnell Douglas, U.S.A.)
Rear-engined, short-to-medium range airliner. Look out for versions with different fuselage lengths. The Series 80 is almost as long as the four-engined DC-8. First flew in 1965, sold over 900 and operated by over 50 airlines.

15

Two-jets

NO CURVE HERE

▲ One-Eleven (British Aerospace, BAC, U.K.)

Similar in size and layout to DC-9 (page 15), but fin is not curved into fuselage and nose is more pointed. Series 500 carries 119 passengers. First service 1965.

Span 28.5m, length 32.61m (Series 500)
Maximum cruising speed 871kph

ENGINES FURTHER FORWARD THAN DC-9 AND ONE-ELEVEN

DORSAL FIN

HIGH TAILPLANE

▲ F.28 Fellowship (Fokker-VFW, Netherlands)

Short-to-medium distance jet airliner. Series 4000, with longest fuselage, carries up to 85 passengers. Engines mounted further forward than on One-Eleven and DC-9 (pages 15 and16), rear fuselage more pointed and there is a dorsal fin. First flight1967.

Span 25.07m, length 29.61m (Series 4000)
Maximum cruising speed 843kp

Two-jets

POINTED FAIRING ON TOP OF FIN

SOME VERSIONS HAVE GLASS NOSE

BULGES STICKING OUT BEHIND WINGS

▲ Tu-134 (Tupolev, U.S.S.R.)
Short-to-medium range airliner similar to DC-9 and One-Eleven (pages 15 and 16). Easily identified, though, by its slim fuselage and bulges sticking out behind wings. Main wheels set wider apart than rivals' and early models have a glass nose for navigator's station.

Span 29m, length 34.9m
Maximum cruising speed 898kph

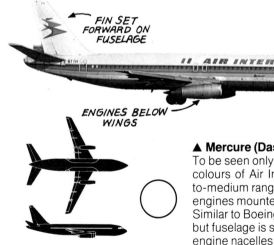

FIN SET FORWARD ON FUSELAGE

ENGINES BELOW WINGS

Span 30.5m, length 33.9m
Maximum cruising speed 926kph

▲ Mercure (Dassault, France)
To be seen only in Europe in the colours of Air Inter airline. Short-to-medium range airliner with engines mounted under wings. Similar to Boeing 737 (page 18), but fuselage is slightly longer and engine nacelles do not stick out behind wings. Entered service 1974, seats 155.

Two-jets

WINGS WELL FORWARD ON FUSELAGE

LARGE ENGINES SLUNG UNDER WINGS

▲ A300 Airbus (Airbus Industrie, International)

Wide-bodied, short-haul airliner built jointly by several countries. Twin engines under the wings which are mounted well forward on the fuselage. Entered service in 1974, carries 336 passengers.

Span 44.8m, length 53.75m
Maximum cruising speed 911kph

SHORT, FAT FUSELAGE

SAME NOSE AS 727

ENGINES STICK OUT BEHIND WINGS

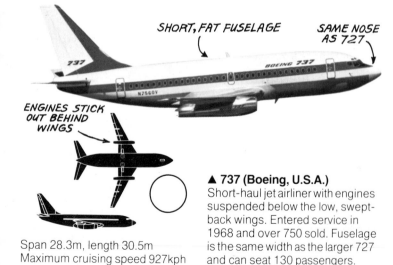

▲ 737 (Boeing, U.S.A.)

Short-haul jet airliner with engines suspended below the low, swept-back wings. Entered service in 1968 and over 750 sold. Fuselage is the same width as the larger 727 and can seat 130 passengers.

Span 28.3m, length 30.5m
Maximum cruising speed 927kph

Two-jets

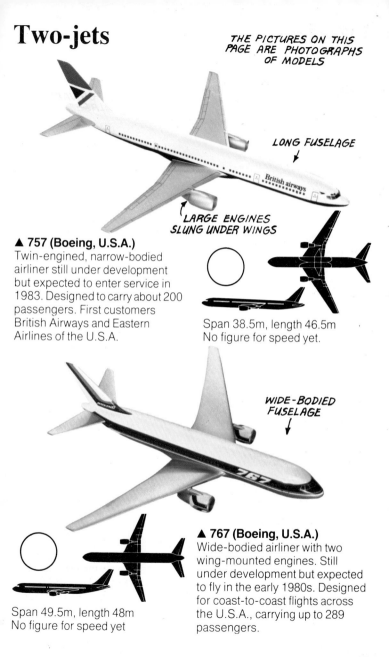

LONG FUSELAGE

LARGE ENGINES SLUNG UNDER WINGS

▲ 757 (Boeing, U.S.A.)

Twin-engined, narrow-bodied airliner still under development but expected to enter service in 1983. Designed to carry about 200 passengers. First customers British Airways and Eastern Airlines of the U.S.A.

Span 38.5m, length 46.5m No figure for speed yet.

WIDE-BODIED FUSELAGE

▲ 767 (Boeing, U.S.A.)

Wide-bodied airliner with two wing-mounted engines. Still under development but expected to fly in the early 1980s. Designed for coast-to-coast flights across the U.S.A., carrying up to 289 passengers.

Span 49.5m, length 48m No figure for speed yet

Turbo-props

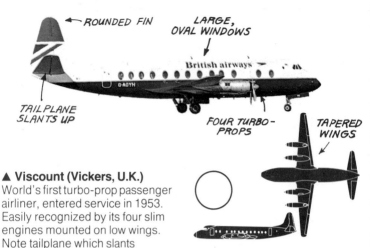

ROUNDED FIN

LARGE, OVAL WINDOWS

British airways

G-AOYN

TAILPLANE SLANTS UP

FOUR TURBO-PROPS

TAPERED WINGS

▲ **Viscount (Vickers, U.K.)**
World's first turbo-prop passenger airliner, entered service in 1953. Easily recognized by its four slim engines mounted on low wings. Note tailplane which slants upwards. Can carry 71 passengers. Total of 444 built and about a quarter still in service.

Span 28.5m, length 26.1m (Series 800)
Maximum cruising speed 567kph

SQUARE-TOPPED FIN

DORSAL FIN

INVICTA INTERNATIONAL

WINGS AND TAILPLANE SLANT UP

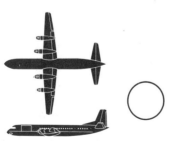

▲ **Vanguard/Merchantman (Vickers, U.K.)**
Passenger version designed to carry up to 139 people on short-distance flights. Merchantman cargo version has large freight door in forward fuselage. Entered service in 1961. Similar layout to Viscount (above) with four engines mounted on tapered wings.

Span 36.1m, length 37.4m
Maximum cruising speed 684kph

Turbo-props

TALLER FIN THAN VANGUARD

RIDGE ON TOP OF FRONT FUSELAGE

DISTINCT "STEP"

▲ IL-18 (Ilyushin, U.S.S.R.)
In the same class as Vanguard (page 20)and Electra (page 23). Has a taller fin than Vanguard and flight deck has a distinct step down to nose area. Entered service in 1959 for medium-range freight and passenger work. Carries up to 122 passengers.

Span 40.1m, length 32.33m
(Series 20)
Maximum cruising speed 607kph

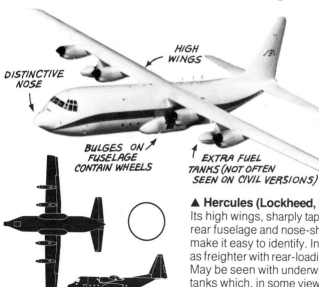

HIGH WINGS

DISTINCTIVE NOSE

BULGES ON FUSELAGE CONTAIN WHEELS

EXTRA FUEL TANKS (NOT OFTEN SEEN ON CIVIL VERSIONS)

Span 37.2m, length 35.8m
Maximum cruising speed 675kph

▲ Hercules (Lockheed, U.S.A.)
Its high wings, sharply tapered rear fuselage and nose-shape make it easy to identify. In service as freighter with rear-loading door. May be seen with underwing fuel tanks which, in some views, make it look like it has six engines. Built in large numbers, particularly for military purposes.

Turbo-props

LARGE SQUARE-
TIPPED FIN →

▲ Britannia (Bristol, U.K.)
Large, medium-to-long range
airliner originally for passenger
services. First flight 1952.
Nicknamed "Whispering Giant"
because it was so quiet. All
surviving aircraft now used for
freight with large door in forward
fuselage.

Span 43m, length 37.8m
(Series 300)
Maximum cruising speed 647kph

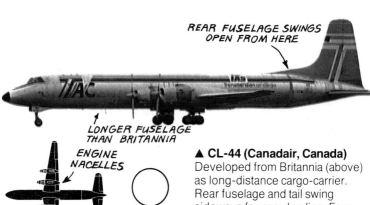

REAR FUSELAGE SWINGS
OPEN FROM HERE

LONGER FUSELAGE
THAN BRITANNIA

ENGINE
NACELLES

▲ CL-44 (Canadair, Canada)
Developed from Britannia (above)
as long-distance cargo-carrier.
Rear fuselage and tail swing
sideways for easy loading. Four
turbo-props on low wings with
engine nacelles sticking out
behind trailing edges. In service
with cargo airlines around the
world.

Span 43m, length 46.3m
Maximum cruising speed 621kph

Turbo-props

FUSELAGE SLOPES
UP FOR REAR LOADING
DOOR

BULGES ON FUSELAGE
CONTAIN WHEELS WHEN
RETRACTED

▲ SC.5 Belfast (Shorts, U.K.)
Looks similar to Hercules, but bigger and less angular. Originally a medium/long range RAF transport plane. First flight 1964. Surviving aircraft converted for use as heavy freight carriers with rear loading doors. Three more due to enter airline service in 1980.

Span 48.4m, length 41.6m
Maximum cruising speed 566kph

LARGE
DORSAL
FIN

TAILPLANE
SLANTS UP

ENGINES
WELL SPACED
ON WING

Span 30.2m, length 31.9m
Maximum cruising speed 652kph

▲ Electra (Lockheed, U.S.A.)
Originally a medium-range airliner for up to 100 passengers. Entered service 1959. Many now converted for freight work with large loading door. The four turbo-props are spaced out on the wings and fin is more curved than on similar aircraft.

23

Turbo-props

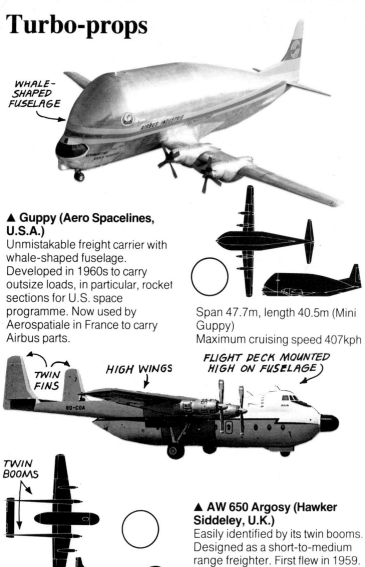

WHALE-SHAPED FUSELAGE

▲ Guppy (Aero Spacelines, U.S.A.)
Unmistakable freight carrier with whale-shaped fuselage. Developed in 1960s to carry outsize loads, in particular, rocket sections for U.S. space programme. Now used by Aerospatiale in France to carry Airbus parts.

Span 47.7m, length 40.5m (Mini Guppy)
Maximum cruising speed 407kph

TWIN FINS

HIGH WINGS

FLIGHT DECK MOUNTED HIGH ON FUSELAGE

TWIN BOOMS

Span 35m, length 26.4m
Maximum cruising speed 453kph

▲ AW 650 Argosy (Hawker Siddeley, U.K.)
Easily identified by its twin booms. Designed as a short-to-medium range freighter. First flew in 1959. Freight hold in centre fuselage with large doors in rear. Some models have a nose opening too. In limited use with cargo airlines.

Turbo-props

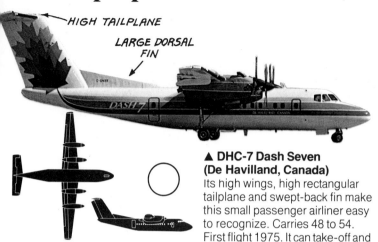

HIGH TAILPLANE

LARGE DORSAL FIN

Span 28.35m, length 24.6m
Maximum cruising speed 452kph

▲ DHC-7 Dash Seven
(De Havilland, Canada)
Its high wings, high rectangular tailplane and swept-back fin make this small passenger airliner easy to recognize. Carries 48 to 54. First flight 1975. It can take-off and land on short runways so look out for it at smaller airstrips.

TALL FIN

MID-TAILPLANE

FIXED UNDERCARRIAGE

▲ DHC-6 Twin Otter
(De Havilland, Canada)
General purpose transport for up to 20 passengers. First flight 1965. Used on local routes and can take-off and land on short airstrips. High wings with two turbo-props. Tailplane set a short way up fin.

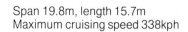

Span 19.8m, length 15.7m
Maximum cruising speed 338kph

Turbo-props

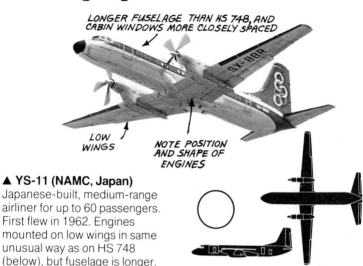

LONGER FUSELAGE THAN HS 748, AND
CABIN WINDOWS MORE CLOSELY SPACED

LOW
WINGS

NOTE POSITION
AND SHAPE OF
ENGINES

▲ YS-11 (NAMC, Japan)

Japanese-built, medium-range
airliner for up to 60 passengers.
First flew in 1962. Engines
mounted on low wings in same
unusual way as on HS 748
(below), but fuselage is longer.
Operates mostly in Far East and
Americas.

Span 31.9m, length 26.3m
Maximum cruising speed 469kph

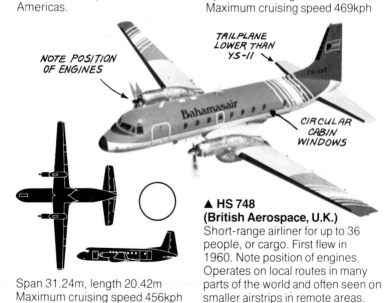

NOTE POSITION
OF ENGINES

TAILPLANE
LOWER THAN
YS-11

CIRCULAR
CABIN
WINDOWS

▲ HS 748
(British Aerospace, U.K.)

Short-range airliner for up to 36
people, or cargo. First flew in
1960. Note position of engines.
Operates on local routes in many
parts of the world and often seen on
smaller airstrips in remote areas.

Span 31.24m, length 20.42m
Maximum cruising speed 456kph

Turbo-props

HIGH WINGS
SLANT UP

BIA IS NOW PART OF
AIR UK (SEE p. 37)

G-APWE

British Island Airways

▲ Herald (Handley Page, U.K.)

Short-range airliner for 44 to 56 passengers. Originally designed with four piston engines, but later changed to twin turbo-props. High wings slant upwards slightly and fin is large and square-cut. Nose slants down steeply from raised flight deck. Now seen mostly in Europe.

Span 28.9m, length 22.9m
Maximum cruising speed 442kph

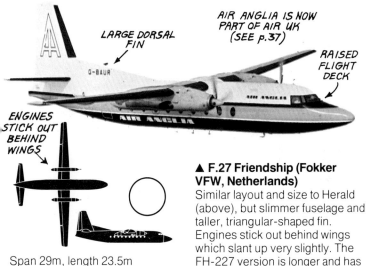

LARGE DORSAL
FIN

AIR ANGLIA IS NOW PART OF AIR UK (SEE p.37)

RAISED FLIGHT DECK

G-BAUR

ENGINES STICK OUT BEHIND WINGS

AIR ANGLIA

Span 29m, length 23.5m
Maximum cruising speed 480kph

▲ F.27 Friendship (Fokker VFW, Netherlands)

Similar layout and size to Herald (above), but slimmer fuselage and taller, triangular-shaped fin. Engines stick out behind wings which slant up very slightly. The FH-227 version is longer and has large cargo door in front fuselage.

Turbo-props

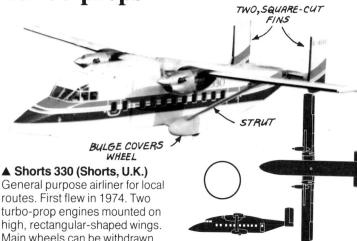

TWO, SQUARE-CUT FINS

STRUT

BULGE COVERS WHEEL

▲ **Shorts 330 (Shorts, U.K.)**
General purpose airliner for local routes. First flew in 1974. Two turbo-prop engines mounted on high, rectangular-shaped wings. Main wheels can be withdrawn into small nacelles which are connected by struts to the wings.

Span 22.76m, length 17.69m
Maximum cruising speed 367kph

SQUARE-CUT FINS

RESCUE

FIXED UNDERCARRIAGE

▲ **SC.7 Skyvan (Shorts, U.K.)**
General purpose transport used particularly on small airstrips in remote areas. First flew in 1963. Straight, narrow wings set on top of square-sided fuselage which slopes sharply upwards at at the back.

Span 19.8m, length 12.2m
Maximum cruising speed 327kph

Turbo-props

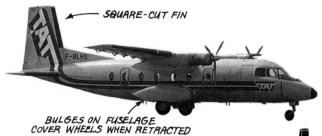

SQUARE-CUT FIN

F-BLHS

BULGES ON FUSELAGE
COVER WHEELS WHEN RETRACTED

▲ Nord 262 (Aerospatiale, France)

Short-range airliner with high wings and two turbo-props. Carries up to 29 passengers and is used frequently on local routes. Bulges on lower fuselage contain wheels when retracted. Tall, square-cut fin.

Span 22.5m, length 19.3m
Maximum cruising speed 396kph

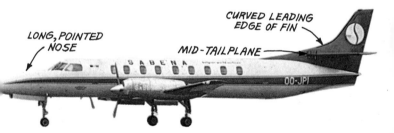

CURVED LEADING
EDGE OF FIN

LONG, POINTED
NOSE

MID-TAILPLANE

OO-JPI

Span 14m, length 18.1m
Maximum cruising speed 473kph

▲ Metro (Swearingen, U.S.A.)

Twin turbo-prop airliner for carrying up to 20 passengers on short local routes. Wings set well forward on slim fuselage. Tailplane mounted a short way up the fin which has a curved leading edge. First flight 1969.

29

Turbo-props

SQUARE WINDOWS

BIA IS NOW PART OF AIR UK (SEE p. 37)

SHORTER NOSE THAN BEECH 99

▲ EMB-110 Bandeirante (Embraer, Brazil)
Small, short-range airliner carrying 15–18 passengers. Twin turbo-props mounted on low wings. Rectangular-shaped, swept-back fin. Entering service in increasing numbers around the world.

Span 15.3m, length 15m
Maximum cruising speed 424kph

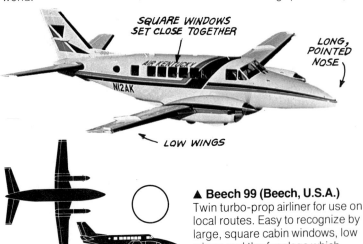

SQUARE WINDOWS SET CLOSE TOGETHER

LONG, POINTED NOSE

N12AK

LOW WINGS

Span 13.9m, length 13.6m
Maximum cruising speed 455kph

▲ Beech 99 (Beech, U.S.A.)
Twin turbo-prop airliner for use on local routes. Easy to recognize by large, square cabin windows, low wings and the fuselage which slopes away from windscreen to give a long, pointed nose.

Piston-engined aircraft

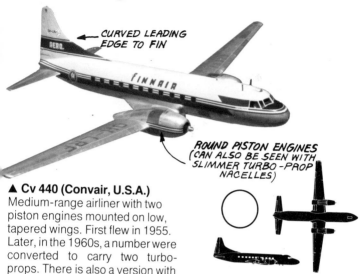

CURVED LEADING EDGE TO FIN

ROUND PISTON ENGINES (CAN ALSO BE SEEN WITH SLIMMER TURBO-PROP NACELLES)

▲ **Cv 440 (Convair, U.S.A.)**
Medium-range airliner with two piston engines mounted on low, tapered wings. First flew in 1955. Later, in the 1960s, a number were converted to carry two turbo-props. There is also a version with a shorter nose. In service for passenger and freight work.

Span 32m, length 24.9m
Maximum cruising speed 483kph

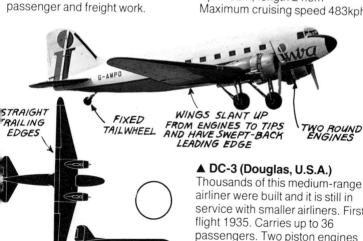

STRAIGHT TRAILING EDGES

FIXED TAILWHEEL

WINGS SLANT UP FROM ENGINES TO TIPS AND HAVE SWEPT-BACK LEADING EDGE

TWO ROUND ENGINES

▲ **DC-3 (Douglas, U.S.A.)**
Thousands of this medium-range airliner were built and it is still in service with smaller airliners. First flight 1935. Carries up to 36 passengers. Two piston engines set on low wings which have straight trailing edges. Wings sweep back and slant up. Fuselage has short, stubby nose.

Span 29m, length 19.65m
Maximum cruising speed 274kph

Piston-engined aircraft

ROUNDED FIN

FOUR ROUND ENGINES

THIS DC-4 HAS UNUSUAL CONTAINER UNDER FUSELAGE

▲ DC-4 (Douglas, U.S.A.)
Medium-range airliner with four piston engines mounted on low wings. First flight 1938. Carries up to 86 passengers or freight. U.K. Carvair version for carrying cars has nose-opening with flight deck perched high on new front fuselage.

Span 35.8m, length 28.62m
Maximum cruising speed 333kph

FUSELAGE SAME SHAPE AS DC-4 BUT LONGER

Span 35.8m, length 32.55m
Maximum cruising speed 583kph

▲ DC-6 (Douglas, U.S.A.)
Developed from the DC-4 for long-range work. First flight 1946. Looks like DC-4 but fuselage is longer. A few still operated for passenger charters, but most now used for freight.

Piston-engined aircraft

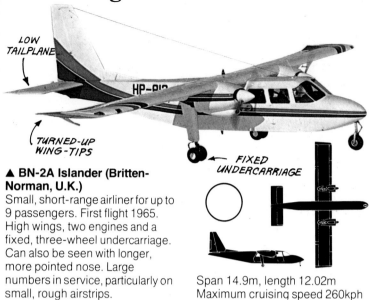

LOW TAILPLANE

TURNED-UP WING-TIPS

FIXED UNDERCARRIAGE

HP-PI?

▲ BN-2A Islander (Britten-Norman, U.K.)

Small, short-range airliner for up to 9 passengers. First flight 1965. High wings, two engines and a fixed, three-wheel undercarriage. Can also be seen with longer, more pointed nose. Large numbers in service, particularly on small, rough airstrips.

Span 14.9m, length 12.02m
Maximum cruising speed 260kph

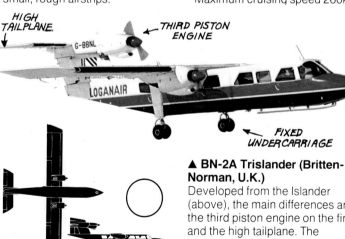

HIGH TAILPLANE

THIRD PISTON ENGINE

G-BBNL

LOGANAIR

FIXED UNDERCARRIAGE

Span 16.1m, length 14.5m
Maximum cruising speed 267kph

▲ BN-2A Trislander (Britten-Norman, U.K.)

Developed from the Islander (above), the main differences are the third piston engine on the fin, and the high tailplane. The fuselage is also longer. First flight 1970. Like the Islander it has large cabin windows and there is also a version with an extra-long nose.

Piston-engined aircraft

SWEPT-BACK FIN

TWO ENGINES WITH FLAT-SIDED NACELLES

ENGINES STICK OUT HERE

▲ **PA-31 Navajo Chieftain (Piper, U.S.A.)**
Small, low-wing airliner for 6–10 passengers. In service on short routes. Fuselage has a fairly long nose and large cabin windows. Engine nacelles have flat upper surface and stick out a short way behind trailing edges of wings.

Span 12.4m, length 10.6m
Maximum cruising speed 407kph

Helicopter

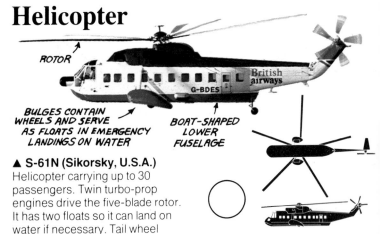

ROTOR

BULGES CONTAIN WHEELS AND SERVE AS FLOATS IN EMERGENCY LANDINGS ON WATER

BOAT-SHAPED LOWER FUSELAGE

▲ **S-61N (Sikorsky, U.S.A.)**
Helicopter carrying up to 30 passengers. Twin turbo-prop engines drive the five-blade rotor. It has two floats so it can land on water if necessary. Tail wheel does not retract. Tail rotor on port side of fin with tailplane on other side.

Rotor diameter 18.95m, length 22.25m
Maximum cruising speed 225kph

Airline spotting

Every airline paints its planes with its own designs and colours. This is called its livery. On the following pages there are pictures of the liveries of 65 of the airlines you are most likely to see, with circles to tick when you spot them. On page 49 there are some outlines of planes for you to colour if you see any other airlines.

The airlines are arranged alphabetically, according to the name as it appears on the plane. To identify an airline, look for the name on the fuselage or fin. If you can not read the name, note the colour of the livery and the design on the fin and see if you can identify the airline from the pictures. The captions give details of where the airline flies to. Scheduled flights are those that the airline operates regularly and charters are special, one-off flights.

Most airlines paint the top of the fuselage white so light and heat reflect off the plane and it does not get too hot.

Much of the plane is often left unpainted so the plane is lighter and can fly faster and use less fuel.

Look out for

National flags painted on the fin or fuselage of the plane.

Airlines which paint their planes in the same colours as their national flag.

Airline names in various scripts and languages.

Airlines

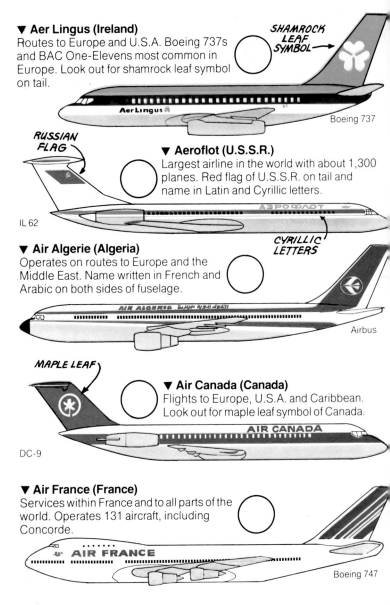

▼ Aer Lingus (Ireland)
Routes to Europe and U.S.A. Boeing 737s and BAC One-Elevens most common in Europe. Look out for shamrock leaf symbol on tail.

SHAMROCK LEAF SYMBOL →

Boeing 737

RUSSIAN FLAG

▼ Aeroflot (U.S.S.R.)
Largest airline in the world with about 1,300 planes. Red flag of U.S.S.R. on tail and name in Latin and Cyrillic letters.

IL 62

CYRILLIC LETTERS

▼ Air Algerie (Algeria)
Operates on routes to Europe and the Middle East. Name written in French and Arabic on both sides of fuselage.

Airbus

MAPLE LEAF

▼ Air Canada (Canada)
Flights to Europe, U.S.A. and Caribbean. Look out for maple leaf symbol of Canada.

DC-9

▼ Air France (France)
Services within France and to all parts of the world. Operates 131 aircraft, including Concorde.

Boeing 747

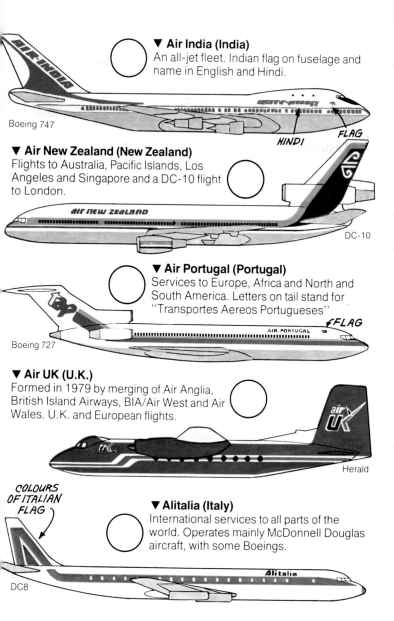

▼ Air India (India)
An all-jet fleet. Indian flag on fuselage and name in English and Hindi.

Boeing 747

HINDI

FLAG

▼ Air New Zealand (New Zealand)
Flights to Australia, Pacific Islands, Los Angeles and Singapore and a DC-10 flight to London.

air new zealand

DC-10

▼ Air Portugal (Portugal)
Services to Europe, Africa and North and South America. Letters on tail stand for "Transportes Aereos Portugueses"

AIR PORTUGAL

FLAG

Boeing 727

▼ Air UK (U.K.)
Formed in 1979 by merging of Air Anglia, British Island Airways, BIA/Air West and Air Wales. U.K. and European flights.

air UK

Herald

COLOURS OF ITALIAN FLAG

▼ Alitalia (Italy)
International services to all parts of the world. Operates mainly McDonnell Douglas aircraft, with some Boeings.

Alitalia

DC8

Airlines

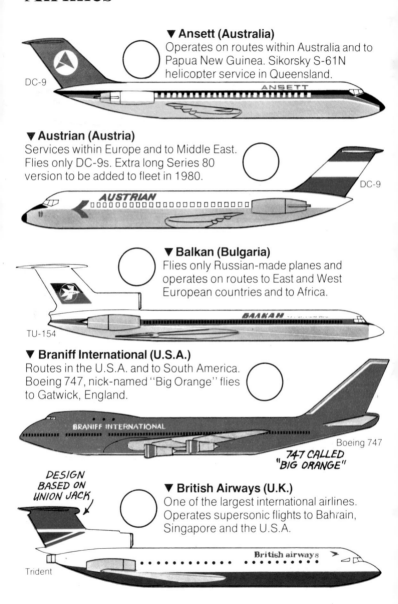

▼ Ansett (Australia)
Operates on routes within Australia and to Papua New Guinea. Sikorsky S-61N helicopter service in Queensland.

DC-9

ANSETT

▼ Austrian (Austria)
Services within Europe and to Middle East. Flies only DC-9s. Extra long Series 80 version to be added to fleet in 1980.

AUSTRIAN

DC-9

▼ Balkan (Bulgaria)
Flies only Russian-made planes and operates on routes to East and West European countries and to Africa.

БАЛКАН

TU-154

▼ Braniff International (U.S.A.)
Routes in the U.S.A. and to South America. Boeing 747, nick-named "Big Orange" flies to Gatwick, England.

BRANIFF INTERNATIONAL

Boeing 747

747 CALLED "BIG ORANGE"

▼ British Airways (U.K.)
One of the largest international airlines. Operates supersonic flights to Bahrain, Singapore and the U.S.A.

DESIGN BASED ON UNION JACK ↙

British airways

Trident

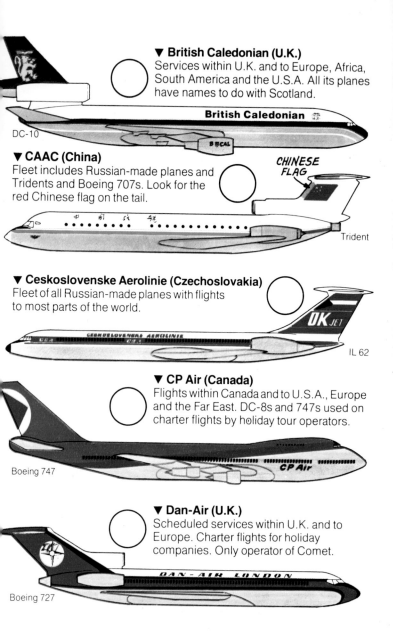

▼ British Caledonian (U.K.)
Services within U.K. and to Europe, Africa, South America and the U.S.A. All its planes have names to do with Scotland.

British Caledonian

DC-10

▼ CAAC (China)
Fleet includes Russian-made planes and Tridents and Boeing 707s. Look for the red Chinese flag on the tail.

CHINESE FLAG

Trident

▼ Ceskoslovenske Aerolinie (Czechoslovakia)
Fleet of all Russian-made planes with flights to most parts of the world.

CESKOSLOVENSKE AEROLINIE

OK JET

IL 62

▼ CP Air (Canada)
Flights within Canada and to U.S.A., Europe and the Far East. DC-8s and 747s used on charter flights by holiday tour operators.

Boeing 747

CP Air

▼ Dan-Air (U.K.)
Scheduled services within U.K. and to Europe. Charter flights for holiday companies. Only operator of Comet.

DAN - AIR LONDON

Boeing 727

39

Airlines

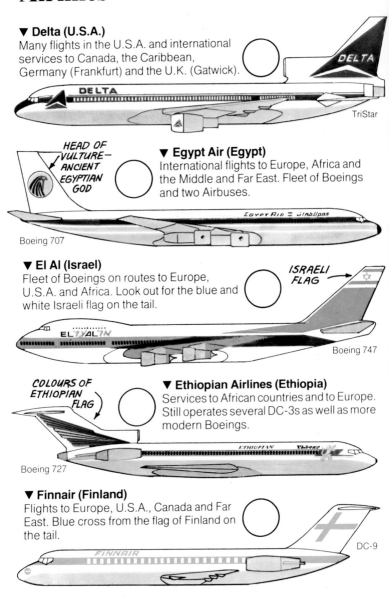

▼ Delta (U.S.A.)
Many flights in the U.S.A. and international services to Canada, the Caribbean, Germany (Frankfurt) and the U.K. (Gatwick).

DELTA

TriStar

HEAD OF VULTURE— ANCIENT EGYPTIAN GOD

▼ Egypt Air (Egypt)
International flights to Europe, Africa and the Middle and Far East. Fleet of Boeings and two Airbuses.

Boeing 707

▼ El Al (Israel)
Fleet of Boeings on routes to Europe, U.S.A. and Africa. Look out for the blue and white Israeli flag on the tail.

ISRAELI FLAG

Boeing 747

COLOURS OF ETHIOPIAN FLAG

▼ Ethiopian Airlines (Ethiopia)
Services to African countries and to Europe. Still operates several DC-3s as well as more modern Boeings.

Boeing 727

▼ Finnair (Finland)
Flights to Europe, U.S.A., Canada and Far East. Blue cross from the flag of Finland on the tail.

DC-9

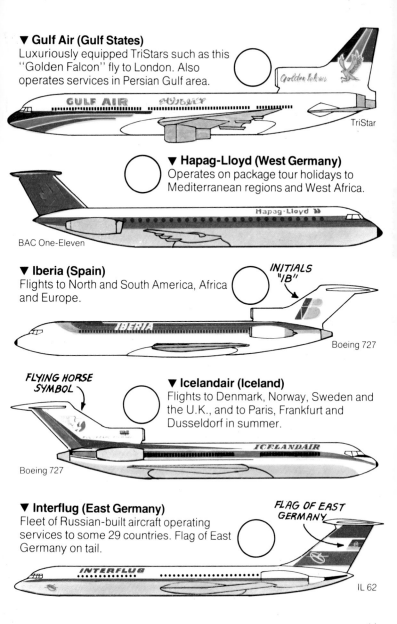

▼ Gulf Air (Gulf States)
Luxuriously equipped TriStars such as this "Golden Falcon" fly to London. Also operates services in Persian Gulf area.

GULF AIR

Golden Falcon

TriStar

▼ Hapag-Lloyd (West Germany)
Operates on package tour holidays to Mediterranean regions and West Africa.

Hapag-Lloyd »

BAC One-Eleven

▼ Iberia (Spain)
Flights to North and South America, Africa and Europe.

INITIALS "IB"

IBERIA

Boeing 727

FLYING HORSE SYMBOL

▼ Icelandair (Iceland)
Flights to Denmark, Norway, Sweden and the U.K., and to Paris, Frankfurt and Dusseldorf in summer.

ICELANDAIR

Boeing 727

▼ Interflug (East Germany)
Fleet of Russian-built aircraft operating services to some 29 countries. Flag of East Germany on tail.

FLAG OF EAST GERMANY

INTERFLUG

IL 62

Airlines

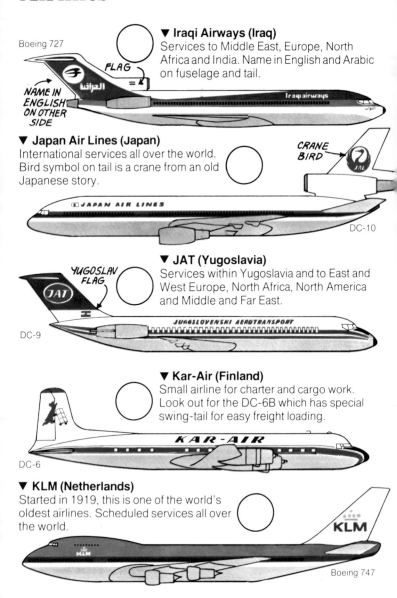

Boeing 727

FLAG

NAME IN ENGLISH ON OTHER SIDE

▼ Iraqi Airways (Iraq)
Services to Middle East, Europe, North Africa and India. Name in English and Arabic on fuselage and tail.

Iraqiairways

▼ Japan Air Lines (Japan)
International services all over the world. Bird symbol on tail is a crane from an old Japanese story.

CRANE BIRD

□ JAPAN AIR LINES

DC-10

▼ JAT (Yugoslavia)
Services within Yugoslavia and to East and West Europe, North Africa, North America and Middle and Far East.

YUGOSLAV FLAG

JUGOSLOVENSKI AEROTRANSPORT

DC-9

▼ Kar-Air (Finland)
Small airline for charter and cargo work. Look out for the DC-6B which has special swing-tail for easy freight loading.

KAR-AIR

DC-6

▼ KLM (Netherlands)
Started in 1919, this is one of the world's oldest airlines. Scheduled services all over the world.

KLM

Boeing 747

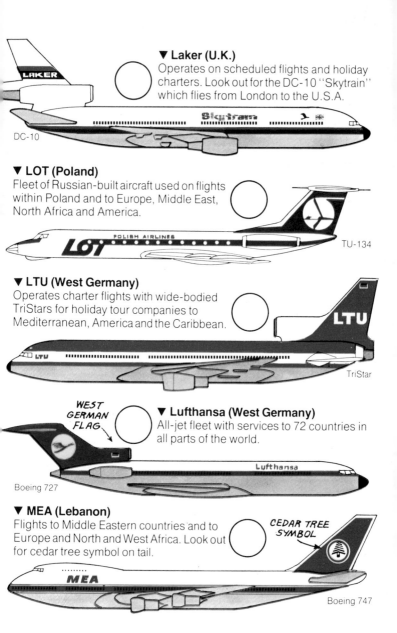

▼ Laker (U.K.)

Operates on scheduled flights and holiday charters. Look out for the DC-10 "Skytrain" which flies from London to the U.S.A.

DC-10

▼ LOT (Poland)

Fleet of Russian-built aircraft used on flights within Poland and to Europe, Middle East, North Africa and America.

POLISH AIRLINES

TU-134

▼ LTU (West Germany)

Operates charter flights with wide-bodied TriStars for holiday tour companies to Mediterranean, America and the Caribbean.

TriStar

WEST GERMAN FLAG

▼ Lufthansa (West Germany)

All-jet fleet with services to 72 countries in all parts of the world.

Boeing 727

▼ MEA (Lebanon)

Flights to Middle Eastern countries and to Europe and North and West Africa. Look out for cedar tree symbol on tail.

CEDAR TREE SYMBOL

Boeing 747

43

Airlines

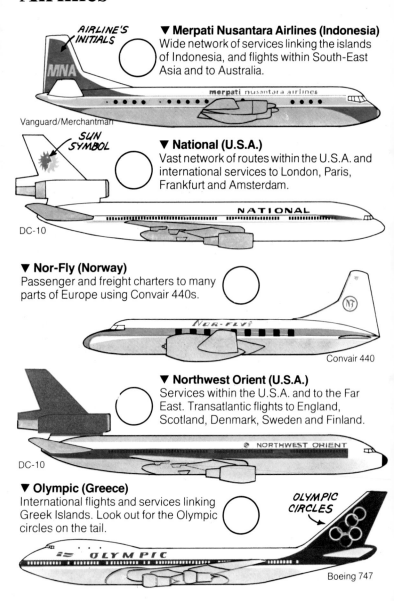

AIRLINE'S INITIALS

▼ **Merpati Nusantara Airlines (Indonesia)**
Wide network of services linking the islands of Indonesia, and flights within South-East Asia and to Australia.

merpati nusantara airlines

Vanguard/Merchantman

SUN SYMBOL

▼ **National (U.S.A.)**
Vast network of routes within the U.S.A. and international services to London, Paris, Frankfurt and Amsterdam.

NATIONAL

DC-10

▼ **Nor-Fly (Norway)**
Passenger and freight charters to many parts of Europe using Convair 440s.

NOR-FLY

Convair 440

▼ **Northwest Orient (U.S.A.)**
Services within the U.S.A. and to the Far East. Transatlantic flights to England, Scotland, Denmark, Sweden and Finland.

NORTHWEST ORIENT

DC-10

▼ **Olympic (Greece)**
International flights and services linking Greek Islands. Look out for the Olympic circles on the tail.

OLYMPIC CIRCLES

OLYMPIC

Boeing 747

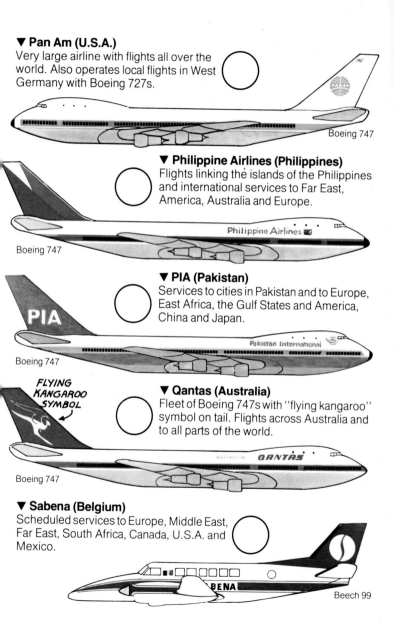

▼ Pan Am (U.S.A.)
Very large airline with flights all over the world. Also operates local flights in West Germany with Boeing 727s.

Boeing 747

▼ Philippine Airlines (Philippines)
Flights linking the islands of the Philippines and international services to Far East, America, Australia and Europe.

Philippine Airlines

Boeing 747

▼ PIA (Pakistan)
Services to cities in Pakistan and to Europe, East Africa, the Gulf States and America, China and Japan.

PIA

Pakistan International

Boeing 747

FLYING KANGAROO SYMBOL

▼ Qantas (Australia)
Fleet of Boeing 747s with "flying kangaroo" symbol on tail. Flights across Australia and to all parts of the world.

QANTAS

Boeing 747

▼ Sabena (Belgium)
Scheduled services to Europe, Middle East, Far East, South Africa, Canada, U.S.A. and Mexico.

BENA

Beech 99

45

Airlines

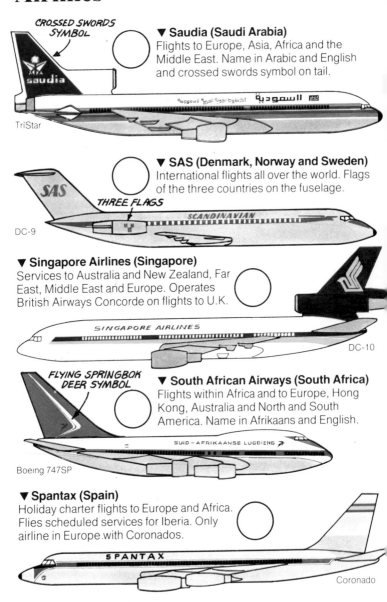

CROSSED SWORDS SYMBOL

▼ **Saudia (Saudi Arabia)**
Flights to Europe, Asia, Africa and the Middle East. Name in Arabic and English and crossed swords symbol on tail.

السعودية ٱلخطوط الجوية العربية السعودية

TriStar

▼ **SAS (Denmark, Norway and Sweden)**
International flights all over the world. Flags of the three countries on the fuselage.

THREE FLAGS

SCANDINAVIAN

DC-9

▼ **Singapore Airlines (Singapore)**
Services to Australia and New Zealand, Far East, Middle East and Europe. Operates British Airways Concorde on flights to U.K.

SINGAPORE AIRLINES

DC-10

FLYING SPRINGBOK DEER SYMBOL

▼ **South African Airways (South Africa)**
Flights within Africa and to Europe, Hong Kong, Australia and North and South America. Name in Afrikaans and English.

SUID – AFRIKAANSE LUGDIENS ➤

Boeing 747SP

▼ **Spantax (Spain)**
Holiday charter flights to Europe and Africa. Flies scheduled services for Iberia. Only airline in Europe with Coronados.

SPANTAX

Coronado

46

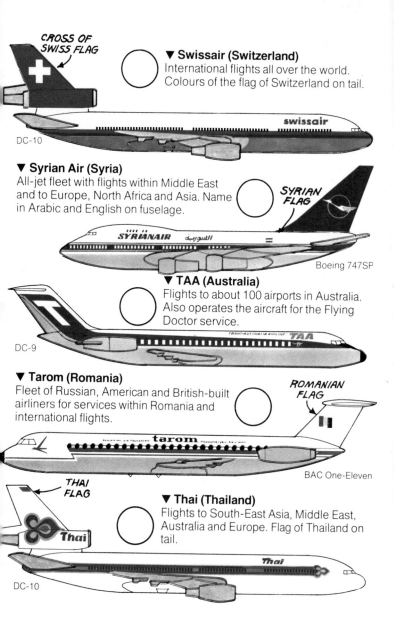

CROSS OF SWISS FLAG

▼ Swissair (Switzerland)
International flights all over the world.
Colours of the flag of Switzerland on tail.

swissair

DC-10

▼ Syrian Air (Syria)
All-jet fleet with flights within Middle East
and to Europe, North Africa and Asia. Name
in Arabic and English on fuselage.

SYRIAN FLAG

SYRIANAIR السورية

Boeing 747SP

▼ TAA (Australia)
Flights to about 100 airports in Australia.
Also operates the aircraft for the Flying
Doctor service.

TRANS-AUSTRALIA AIRLINE TAA

DC-9

▼ Tarom (Romania)
Fleet of Russian, American and British-built
airliners for services within Romania and
international flights.

ROMANIAN FLAG

tarom

BAC One-Eleven

THAI FLAG

▼ Thai (Thailand)
Flights to South-East Asia, Middle East,
Australia and Europe. Flag of Thailand on
tail.

Thai

Thai

DC-10

47

Airlines

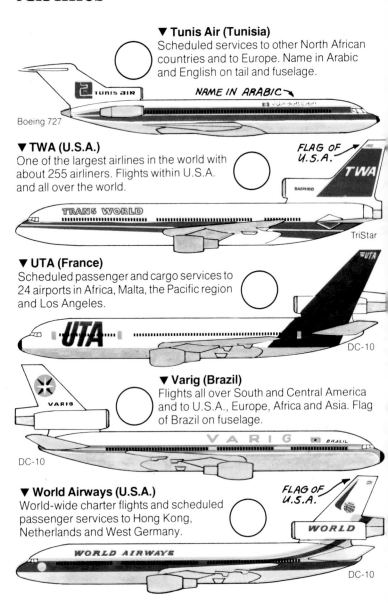

▼ Tunis Air (Tunisia)
Scheduled services to other North African countries and to Europe. Name in Arabic and English on tail and fuselage.

NAME IN ARABIC →

Boeing 727

▼ TWA (U.S.A.)
One of the largest airlines in the world with about 255 airliners. Flights within U.S.A. and all over the world.

FLAG OF U.S.A.

TriStar

▼ UTA (France)
Scheduled passenger and cargo services to 24 airports in Africa, Malta, the Pacific region and Los Angeles.

DC-10

▼ Varig (Brazil)
Flights all over South and Central America and to U.S.A., Europe, Africa and Asia. Flag of Brazil on fuselage.

DC-10

▼ World Airways (U.S.A.)
World-wide charter flights and scheduled passenger services to Hong Kong, Netherlands and West Germany.

FLAG OF U.S.A.

DC-10

Airlines

If you see an airline not shown in this book you can fill in one of these outlines in the colour of its livery. Write the name of the airline on the dotted line next to the picture.

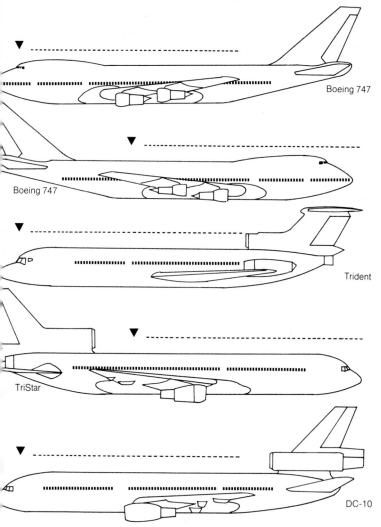

▼ --

Boeing 747

▼ --

Boeing 747

▼ --

Trident

▼ --

TriStar

▼ --

DC-10

At an airport

An airport can be anything from a field with a short, grassy runway, to a vast international airport covering many square kilometres. These two pages show some of the things to look out for at a large, busy airport.

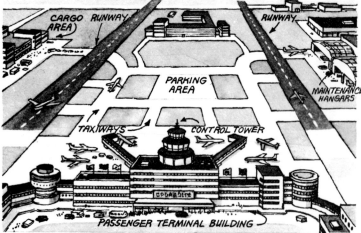

A large airport usually has two runways so planes can take-off and land at the same time. The runways are numbered, and this number also shows their compass bearing. For instance, runway 25 has a compass bearing of 250°. This system is used all over the world. Nowadays planes do not need very long runways and the maximum length is about four kilometres.

Control tower

Staff with radar and radio equipment direct planes on the ground and in the air.

Taxiways

These link runways with terminals. Staff with orange bats guide the pilot.

Airbridges

These are passages which are extended to link the plane with the terminal.

Servicing a plane

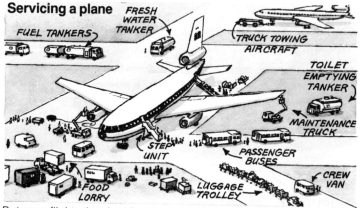

Between flights the plane has to be refuelled, cleaned and stocked with food, and regular maintenance checks are carried out. These are some of the vehicles you will see on the taxiways.

Airport staff

PILOTS

STEWARDESSES AND STEWARDS

ENGINEER   GROUND STAFF TO GUIDE PILOT

Airport facts

⭐ The busiest airport in the world is Chicago O'Hare. Over 45 million passengers pass through every year, and over three quarters of a million aircraft take off and land there every year.

⭐ The airport which covers the largest area is Fort Worth in Dallas, U.S.A. It covers nearly 80sq km.

⭐ The largest passenger aircraft is the Boeing 747 "Jumbo jet" which can carry up to 500 passengers.

Fleet lists

The chart on this page and pages 54–55 shows which of the aircraft in this book each of the airlines operates*.

	707	720	747	747SP	IL-62	VC10	Coronado	Comet	DC-8 Srs 10-50	DC-8 Srs 60	Concorde	DC-10	Trident
Aer Lingus	✈		✈										
Aeroflot					✈								
Air Algerie													
Air Canada			✈						✈	✈			
Air France	✈		✈								✈		
Air India	✈		✈										
Air New Zealand									✈			✈	
Air Portugal	✈		✈										
Air UK													
Alitalia			✈							✈		✈	
Ansett													
Austrian													
Balkan													
Braniff			✈	✈					✈	✈	✈		
British Airways	✈		✈			✈					✈		✈
British Caledonian	✈											✈	
CAAC	✈			✈	✈								✈
Ceskoslovenske					✈								
CP Air			✈						✈	✈		✈	
Dan Air								✈					
Delta									✈	✈			
Egypt Air	✈												
El Al	✈	✈	✈										
Ethiopian Airlines	✈	✈											
Finnair										✈		✈	
Gulf Air													
Hapag Lloyd													
Iberia			✈						✈	✈		✈	
Icelandair													
Interflug					✈								
Iraqi Airways	✈		✈										✈
Japan Air Lines			✈						✈	✈		✈	

*Aircraft not used by any of the airlines in the book are not in the chart.

727	Tu-154	TriStar	Yak-40	Caravelle	DC-9	One-Eleven	Fellowship	Tu-134	Airbus	737	Other aircraft — Turbo-prop and piston-engined aircraft owned by each airline.
					✈					✈	
	✈		✈				✈				IL-18
✈										✈	Nord 262
✈		✈		✈							
✈			✈			✈		✈			Friendship
										✈	Friendship
✈											
						✈	✈				Herald, Friendship, Bandeirante, Chieftain
✈					✈						
✈					✈						Electra, Friendship, S-61N
					✈						
	✈		✈				✈				IL-18
✈											
		✈			✈					✈	Viscount, HS 748, S-61N
					✈						S-61N, Chieftain
											Viscount, IL-18, Twin Otter
			✈				✈				IL-18
✈										✈	
✈					✈						Viscount, HS 748
✈	✈			✈							
								✈	✈		
✈											DC-3
			✈	✈							Convair 440
	✈									✈	Friendship, Shorts 330, Islander, Chieftain
✈					✈			✈			
✈				✈							Friendship
✈											Friendship
								✈			IL-18
✈										✈	
✈											

Fleet lists

	707	720	747	747SP	IL-62	VC10	Coronado	Comet	DC-8 Srs 10–50	DC-8 Srs 60	Concorde	DC-10	Trident
JAT	✈											✈	
Kar Air									✈				
KLM			✈						✈	✈		✈	
Laker	✈											✈	
LOT					✈								
LTU													
Lufthansa	✈		✈									✈	
MEA	✈	✈	✈										
Merpati Nusantara	✈												
National												✈	
Nor-Fly													
Northwest Orient			✈									✈	
Olympic	✈	✈	✈										
Pan Am	✈		✈	✈									
Philippine Airlines			✈						✈			✈	
PIA	✈	✈	✈									✈	
Qantas			✈										
Sabena	✈		✈									✈	
Saudia	✈	✈	✈							✈			
SAS			✈							✈		✈	
Singapore Airlines	✈		✈								✈	✈	
South African	✈		✈	✈									
Spantax						✈				✈		✈	
Swissair			✈							✈		✈	
Syrian Air				✈									
TAA													
Tarom	✈				✈								
Thai			✈							✈		✈	
Tunis Air													
TWA	✈		✈	✈									
UTA			✈						✈	✈		✈	
Varig	✈											✈	
World Airways			✈							✈		✈	

727	Tu-154	TriStar	Yak-40	Caravelle	DC-9	One-Eleven	Fellowship	Tu-134	Airbus	737	Other aircraft — Turbo-prop and piston-engined aircraft owned by each airline.
✈				✈							
											Twin Otter, Bandeirante, DC-3, DC-6
					✈						
						✈					
								✈			IL-18
		✈									
✈									✈	✈	
✈											Viscount, Vanguard, Twin Otter, HS 748, Friendship, DC-3
											Convair 440
✈											
✈									✈	✈	YS-11, Skyvan, Islander
✈		✈									
							✈	✈			Argosy, YS-11, HS 748, DC-3, Islander
								✈			Friendship
										✈	Metro, Beech 99
✈		✈								✈	
					✈			✈			
✈										✈	
✈									✈	✈	HS 748
					✈						Dash Seven, Twin Otter
					✈						
✈			✈								DC-6
✈					✈						Twin Otter, Friendship
	✈					✈					IL-18
									✈		
✈										✈	
✈		✈		✈							
✈									✈		Electra
✈											

Registration numbers

All civil aircraft have a registration number painted on the tail or fuselage. The first part of the number shows which country the aircraft is registered in and the rest of the number is different for each plane. If you keep a record of the registration numbers of planes you spot, you will know if you see the same plane again. To find out which country a plane is registered in, look up the first part of the number in this list. The registrations which begin with a letter are listed first, alphabetically, and those which begin with a number are afterwards in numerical order.

A2-	Botswana	H4-	Solomon Islands
A6-	United Arab Emirates	HA-	Hungary
		HB-	Switzerland and Liechtenstein
A7-	Qatar	HC-	Ecuador
A9-	Bahrain	HH-	Haiti
A40-	Oman	HI-	Dominican Republic
AN-	Nicaragua		
AP-	Pakistan	HK-	Colombia
B-	China	HL-	South Korea
C-	Canada	HMAY-	Mongolia
C2-	Nauru	HP-	Panama
C5-	Gambia	HR-	Honduras
C6-	Bahamas	HS-	Thailand
C9-	Mozambique	HZ-	Saudi Arabia
CC-	Chile	I-	Italy
CCCP-	U.S.S.R.	J5-	Guinea Bissau
CF-	Canada	JA-	Japan
CN-	Morocco	JY-	Jordan
CP-	Bolivia	LN-	Norway
CS-	Portugal	LQ-, LV-	Argentina
CU-	Cuba	LX-	Luxembourg
CX-	Uruguay	LZ-	Bulgaria
D-	West Germany	N-	U.S.A.
D2-	Angola	OB-	Peru
D6	Comoros Islands	OD-	Lebanon
DM-	East Germany	OE-	Austria
DQ-	Fiji	OH-	Finland
EC-	Spain	OK-	Czechoslovakia
EI, EJ-	Ireland	OO-	Belgium
EL-	Liberia	OY-	Denmark
EP-	Iran	P-	North Korea
ET-	Ethiopia	P2-	Papua New Guinea
F-	France		
G-	United Kingdom		

PH-	Netherlands	YV-	Venezuela
PK-	Indonesia and West Irian	ZA-	Albania
		ZK-, ZL-, ZM-	New Zealand
PP-, PT-	Brazil	ZP-	Paraguay
PZ-	Surinam	ZS-, ZT-, ZU-	South Africa
RDPL-	Laos	3A-	Monaco
RP-	Philippines	3B-	Mauritius
S2-	Bangladesh	3C-	Equatorial Guinea
S7-	Seychelles	3D-	Swaziland
S9-	Sao Tomé	3X-	Guinea
SE-	Sweden	4R-	Sri Lanka
SP-	Poland	4W-	North Yemen
ST-	Sudan	4X-	Israel
SU-	Egypt	5A-	Libya
SX-	Greece	5B-	Cyprus
TC-	Turkey	5H-	Tanzania
TF-	Iceland	5N-	Nigeria
TG-	Guatemala	5R-	Madagascar
TI-	Costa Rica	5T-	Mauritania
TJ-	Cameroon	5U-	Niger
TL-	Central African Republic	5V-	Togo
		5W-	Western Samoa
TN-	Congo	5X-	Uganda
TR-	Gabon	5Y-	Kenya
TS-	Tunisia	60-	Somalia
TT-	Chad	6V-, 6W-	Senegal
TU-	Ivory Coast	6Y-	Jamaica
TY-	Benin	70-	South Yemen
TZ-	Mali	7P-	Lesotho
VH-	Australia	7Q-	Malawi
VN-	Vietnam	7T-	Algeria
VP-V	St Vincent	8P-	Barbados
VP-Y, VP-W	Zimbabwe Rhodesia	8Q-	Maldive Islands
		8R-	Guyana
VQ-G	Grenada	9G-	Ghana
VQ-L	St Lucia	9H-	Malta
VT-	India	9J	Zambia
XA, XB-, XC-	Mexico	9K-	Kuwait
XT-	Upper Volta	9L-	Sierra Leone
XU-	Kampuchea	9M-	Malaysia
XY-, XZ-	Burma	9N-	Nepal
YA-	Afghanistan	9Q-	Zaïre
YI-	Iraq	9U-	Burundi
YK-	Syria	9V-	Singapore
YR-	Romania	9XR-	Ruanda
YS-	El Salvador	9Y-	Trinidad and Tobago
YU-	Yugoslavia		

Airliners scorecard

When you spot a plane you can fill in its details on this scorecard.
Next to the type of plane you saw, write the name of the airline,
the date, and if possible, the registration number. The planes are
listed in the same order as in this book.

Page	Airliner	Score	Airline	Registration Number	Date
6	Boeing 707	5			
6	Boeing 720	10			
7	Boeing 747	5			
7	Boeing 747SP	20			
8	IL-62	15			
8	VC-10	20			
9	Coronado	20			
9	Comet	25			
10	DC-8 (Srs 10-50)	15			
10	DC-8 (Srs 60)	15			
11	Concorde	15			
11	BAe 146	25			
12	Trident	5			
12	Boeing 727	5			
13	Tu-154	15			
13	TriStar	15			
14	DC-10	15			
14	YAK-40	25			
15	Caravelle	10			
15	DC-9	5			
16	One-Eleven	5			
16	Fellowship	15			
17	Tu-134	15			
17	Mercure	20			
18	Airbus	10			
18	Boeing 737	5			

Page	Airliner	Score	Airline	Registration Number	Date
19	Boeing 757	25			
19	Boeing 767	25			
20	Viscount	10			
20	Vanguard	20			
21	IL-18	25			
21	Hercules	15			
22	Britannia	20			
22	CL-44	15			
23	Belfast	25			
23	Electra	25			
24	Guppy	25			
24	Argosy	20			
25	Dash Seven	25			
25	Twin Otter	15			
26	YS-11	25			
26	HS 748	10			
27	Herald	10			
27	Friendship	10			
28	Shorts 330	20			
28	Skyvan	20			
29	Nord 262	15			
29	Metro	15			
30	Bandeirante	10			
30	Beech 99	15			
31	Convair 440	25			
31	DC-3	15			
32	DC-4	25			
32	DC-6	20			
33	Islander	5			
33	Trislander	10			
34	Chieftain	10			
34	Sikorsky S-61N	15			

Airlines scorecard

On this scorecard you can keep a record of the airlines you see. Next to the name of the airline, write the name of the aircraft, the registration number, if you can see it, and the date. The airlines are arranged in alphabetical order. If you see any other airlines you can fill in their names at the end of the scorecard.

Airline	Score	Airliner	Registration Number	Date
Aer Lingus	5			
Aeroflot	15			
Air Algerie	20			
Air Canada	10			
Air France	5			
Air India	15			
Air New Zealand	20*			
Air Portugal	15			
Air UK	5			
Alitalia	10			
Ansett	5			
Austrian	15			
Balkan	10			
Braniff	20			
British Airways	5			
British Caledonian	5			
CAAC	20			
Ceskoslovenske	15			
CP Air	15			
Dan Air	5			
Delta	15			
Egypt Air	15			
El Al	10			
Ethiopian	20			
Finnair	10			
Gulf Air	10			
Hapag Lloyd	20			
Iberia	10			
Icelandair	15			
Interflug	20			
Iraqi Airways	15			
Japan Air Lines	15*			

*Score only 5 points if seen in Australia

Airline	Score	Airliner	Registration Number	Date
JAT	10			
Kar Air	20			
KLM	5			
Laker	5			
LOT	15			
LTU	20			
Lufthansa	5			
MEA	10			
Merpati Nusantara	25			
National	20			
Nor-Fly	20			
Northwest Orient	15			
Olympic	10			
Pan Am	5			
Philippine Airlines	20*			
PIA	15			
Qantas	5			
Sabena	5			
Saudia	15			
SAS	5			
Singapore Airlines	15*			
South African	15			
Spantax	10			
Swissair	5			
Syrian Air	15			
TAA	5			
Tarom	10			
Thai	20*			
Tunis Air	15			
TWA	5			
UTA	20			
Varig	15			
World Airways	15			

Score only 5 points if seen in Australia

Name the planes game

Can you recognize these planes? Note the type of engines they have, and where they are positioned, and the shape of the nose, wings and fin. All the planes are in this book, but if you get stuck, the answers are on page 64.

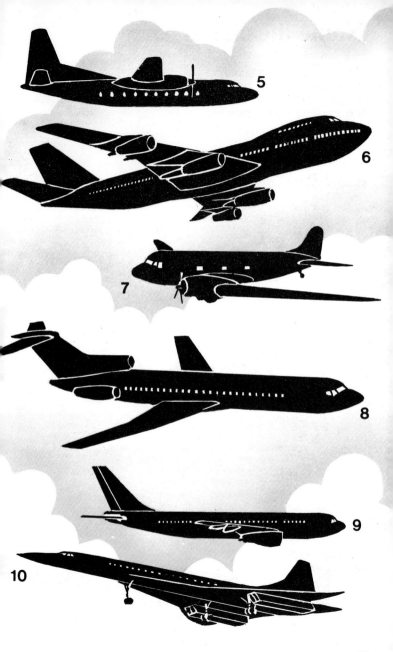

5

6

7

8

9

10

Index

Game answers: 1. DC-10; 2. TriStar; 3. Herald; 4. One-Eleven; 5. Friendship; 6. Boeing 747; 7. DC-3; 8. Boeing 727; 9. Airbus; 10. Concorde.